THIS IS YOUR WORLD

THE STORY OF Bob Ross®

Written by Sophia Gholz

Illustrated by Robin Boyden

RP|KIDS

PHILADELPHIA

Running Press Kids
Hachette Book Group
1290 Avenue of the Americas, New York, NY 10104
www.runningpress.com/rpkids
@RP_Kids

Printed in China

First Edition: September 2021

Published by Running Press Kids, an imprint of Perseus Books, LLC,
a subsidiary of Hachette Book Group, Inc. The Running Press Kids
name and logo is a trademark of the Hachette Book Group.

The Hachette Speakers Bureau provides a wide range of authors for
speaking events. To find out more, go to www.hachettespeakersbureau.com
or call (866) 376-6591.

The publisher is not responsible for websites (or their content)
that are not owned by the publisher.

Text written by Sophia Gholz.
Illustrations by Robin Boyden.

Print book cover and interior design by Marissa Raybuck.

Library of Congress Control Number: 2020944747

ISBNs: 978-0-7624-7356-4 (hardcover), 978-0-7624-7355-7 (ebook),
978-0-7624-7453-0 (ebook), 978-0-7624-7452-3 (ebook)

1010

10 9 8 7 6 5 4 3 2 1

For my mom, and for all the creatives in the world.
There is an artist in everyone.
— S. G.

For Grampy.
— R. B.

"*Hello . . . ready to paint a fantastic picture with me?*
The only guideline we use . . . is our imagination."

—BOB ROSS

This is artist and television star, Bob Ross.
In his lifetime, he created more than 30,000 paintings.
Yet, you won't see them hanging next to the *Mona Lisa* or paired with Pablo Picasso.
But that never bothered Bob; he didn't paint for fame or fortune.

Growing up in Florida in the 1940s, Bob Ross lived a simple life and found joy in simple things, like the clouds and trees. His heart was connected to the nature around him, and his house was often filled with the injured wildlife he rescued.

"You need to understand nature to appreciate the great, great things that have been created. We spend so much of our life walking around looking, but never, never seeing . . ."

Bob saw everything.

Phthalo Blue!

Sap Green!

Cadmium Yellow!

As a boy, he spent time working with his father, a carpenter. He taught Bob to build sheds of Dark Sienna and barns in Van Dyke Brown and Yellow Ochre.

Bob loved creating, but building was hard work.
One day, Bob lost the tip of a finger in a carpentry accident.

"We don't make mistakes, in our world,
we only have happy accidents.
And very, very quickly we learn to work
with anything that happens . . ."

And he learned.

Before he owned his first set of paints,
Bob learned to create with his imagination—
his eyes never drifting far from the clouds.

He'd lay in the grass and see
shapes floating across the sky.

Perhaps Bob dreamed of seeing those clouds up close, because in 1961, at eighteen years old, he enlisted in the United States Air Force.

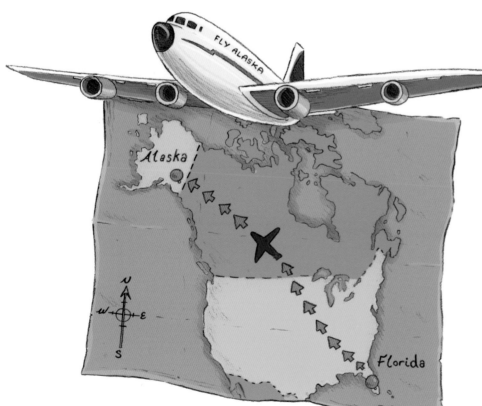

But Bob didn't become a pilot who soared through the clouds. Instead, he was sent far away from Florida to Fairbanks, Alaska.

The Alaskan landscape was like nothing he had ever seen before.
Titanium White!
Indian Yellow!
Midnight Black!

In the Air Force, Bob discovered the power of words.
As a sergeant, he spent his days barking orders.

"Make your beds!"
"Stand up tall!"
"Don't be late!"

And the soldiers listened.

But Bob didn't like to yell. He was happiest in nature, and he escaped to the quiet countryside whenever he could— his heart bursting to share what he saw with others.

When the Air Force announced
it was hosting a painting class,
Bob eagerly enrolled, hoping to paint
the images that swirled inside him.

But he became discouraged
by his teachers.

*"They'd tell you what makes a tree,
but they wouldn't tell you
how to paint a tree."*

Bob spent hours agonizing over details on his canvas.
The traditional style of painting couldn't capture his heart.
There had to be a different way.

Then one day, powerful words drifted from a television set over the din of a crowded room.
"How long can you hold the dream?" said Bill Alexander, a painter on TV.
Bob felt like Bill was talking directly to him.

Bill skillfully spread paint across a canvas in a technique called *alla prima*,
where wet oil paint is used without allowing it to dry between layers.
Landscapes flashed through Bob's mind. This was it!

Bob began to paint in every spare moment. Now he explored the countryside through art.
During lunch breaks he'd hold a sandwich in one hand and a brush in the other.
He practiced using the wet-on-wet style until he became so fast that
he could finish a whole painting in thirty minutes.

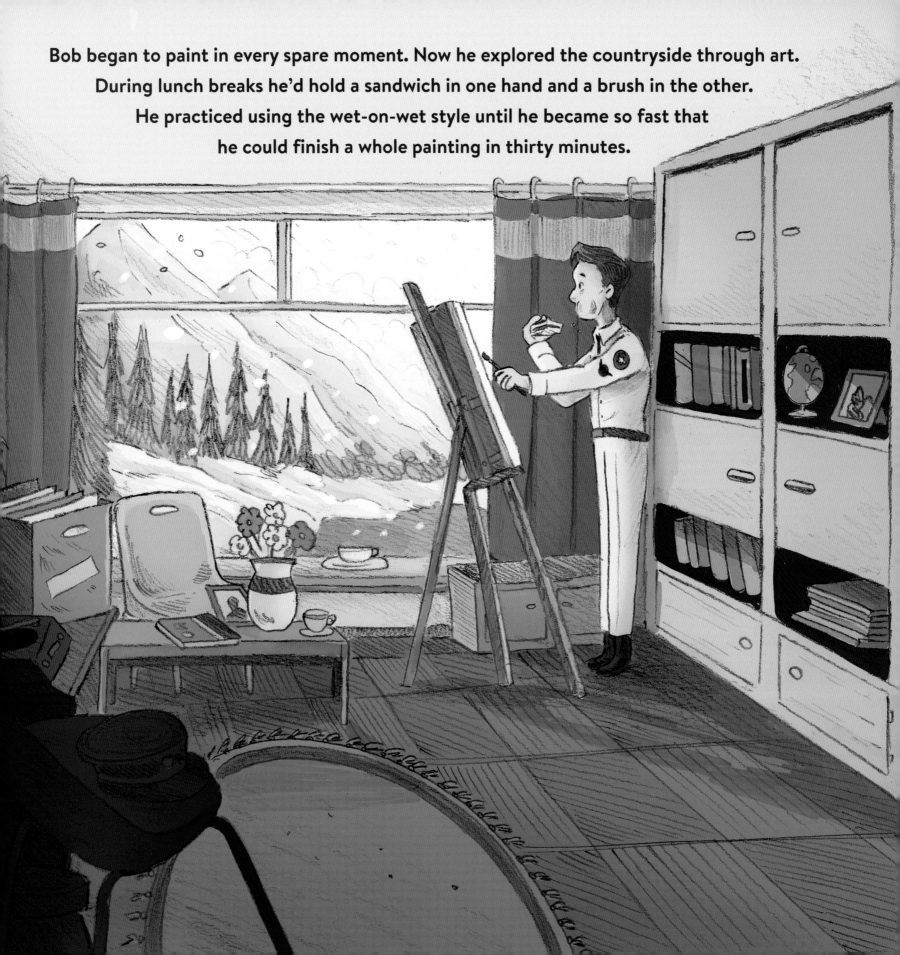

Van Dyke Brown!

Bright Red!

Alizarin Crimson!

For the first time, Bob's art flowed freely from his heart.

But Bob yearned for more. If he could learn to capture
his heart in paint, others could too, and he wanted to help.
Bob retired from the military and left Alaska behind.

He sought out Bill Alexander,
the painter from TV.

Bob met Bill for the first time and
learned more about painting *alla prima*.
He studied hard and, before long, he was
leading painting workshops for Bill.

Now, instead of barking orders, Bob taught with a soft voice.
His gentle and encouraging words held power.

*"Just let your imagination be your guide.
Let it happen. . . . Believe in yourself.
Believe in what you can do."*

And his students listened.

In one of his classes, a student named Annette sat behind a canvas.
She'd been suffering from a deep sadness,
but Bob's words of encouragement lifted her heart.

"Painting—painting offers freedom.
On this canvas you can move mountains.
You can do anything on this canvas."

Annette knew that if Bob's words could help her, others might like to hear them too.
Bob and Annette became business partners, along with Bob's wife, Jane,
and Annette's husband, Walter; they took care of the office work.

Soon, Bob was traveling all over the country, teaching the "Bob Ross Technique" of painting in malls and small shops.

At first, his classes were empty.
No one had heard of Bob Ross before.

But that didn't bother him.
If only one person showed up, he taught them.

"To me the first step in accomplishing anything is to believe that you can do it."

And Bob believed.

In 1982, Annette sent a videotape of Bob painting to a public television station.
Bob's words and fast technique caught the eye of the station's manager.
They offered to feature Bob on his own television show. He was thrilled!
Now he could share his joy of painting with everyone.

Episode 1 of *The Joy of Painting* debuted on public television in 1983.

*"Hello, I'm Bob Ross. . . .
I'll be your host as we experience
The Joy of Painting."*

It was a simple studio set. But that didn't bother Bob.
He found joy in simple things, like the same paints and techniques
he used in every episode so viewers at home could follow along easily.

Bob hoped his viewers would find courage in art.

"Be brave.
This is your bravery test.
We'll just have us a big tree
that lives right there.
We'll give him a friend.
Have two big trees . . ."

"You can fix anything now. Because you are the master. The master.
You have unlimited power on this canvas . . ."

"It's a super nice example of what can be done with just a few colors,
a little imagination, and a happy dream in your heart."

*"Don't worry about
what you're going to paint,
just start painting."*

*"Now. Let's build,
let's build some happy
little things here."*

*"All you need is a dream in your heart
and the desire to put it on canvas."*

And the world listened.

Over the next 11 years,
Bob taped 403 episodes
of *The Joy of Painting*.

Some people claimed
Bob wasn't a true artist because
his techniques were different.

Others said Bob's soft voice
put them to sleep.

But that never bothered Bob. He didn't paint for fame or fortune;
Bob was a teacher and his lessons went far beyond the simple joy of painting.

"On this canvas, you're the creator. Anything that you want,
you can build here. This is your world . . ."

AUTHOR'S NOTE

Bob may have been known as an artist, but his magic lay in his words. In each episode of *The Joy of Painting*, Bob encouraged and cheered for the viewer at home. His message was clear: be brave, believe in yourself, it's okay to make mistakes, and, most of all, individuality is good—we won't all see the same thing when we look at the mountains, and that is okay. Despite his massive popularity, Bob was rarely interviewed and little is shared about his early life. However, while researching this book, I learned that Bob often told short stories on his show while he painted. One of my favorites is this one:

"We have a lot of requests that have come in wanting portraits. And years ago, I studied with a super painter and studied portraits for oh, maybe a year and a half, two years, and he became a very dear friend. And he took me aside one night and he says, 'Bob, I've got to tell you the truth.' He said, 'I want you to go and paint bushes and trees because that's where your heart is and give up portraits.'"

Like many creative people, Bob had to experiment in order to find his artistic voice. His art didn't come easily at first, and that's an important lesson to learn as an artist. Art takes work. As Bob said,

"Talent is a pursued interest . . . anything that you're willing to practice, you can do."

MORE ABOUT BOB ROSS

Robert Norman Ross was born in Daytona, Florida, on October 29, 1942. His love of nature and animals was evident from the start, when he rescued injured wildlife as a child. Later in his adult life, Bob would become well known as an environmentalist and animal activist. During his last season of *The Joy of Painting*, Bob featured many animal guests, including Peapod, his pocket squirrel, whom Bob rescued as a baby.

During his career with the United States Air Force, Bob reached the rank of Master Sergeant. When he retired from the military in 1981, Bob swore he'd never bark another order again. He spent the rest of his life focused on sharing the joy of painting.

Early on as a painter, Bob struggled to find his artistic style. In many episodes of *The Joy of Painting*, Bob referred to spending hours agonizing over details using the traditional style of painting. It wasn't until he discovered the *alla prima* (wet-on-wet) technique that Bob was able to finally express himself artistically. He eventually became so skilled with his style that he could film an entire season of *The Joy of Painting* in just three days, taping four to seven episodes a day. This allowed Bob to spend most of his time teaching and certifying others to teach The Bob Ross Technique around the world. Over the course of filming, Bob is said to have created more than 30,000 paintings, but he didn't sell them. Instead, he donated them to charities and public television stations to raise money. Bob was never paid for appearing on his television show, either.

On July 4, 1995, Bob Ross died of lymphoma in Orlando, Florida. He was fifty-two years old.

MORE ABOUT *THE JOY OF PAINTING*

In total, *The Joy of Painting* aired 403 episodes across 31 seasons from 1983 to 1994. By 1995, Bob's show was being viewed internationally in more than fifteen countries and in over ninety-million homes across America. Decades after Bob Ross first appeared on public television, his encouraging words and painting lessons are still inspiring millions of people. You can still find *The Joy of Painting* on public television and on streaming platforms today.

"I want to wish you the absolute every possible joy that life can bring."

—BOB ROSS

BOB'S PAINTING COLORS

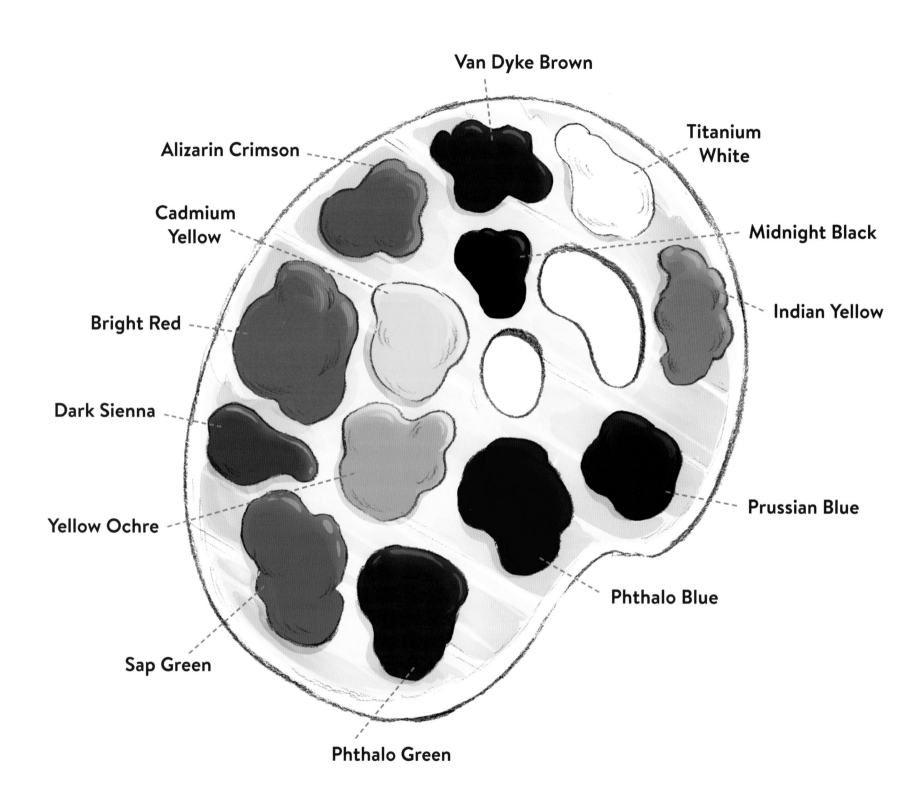

Van Dyke Brown

Titanium White

Alizarin Crimson

Cadmium Yellow

Midnight Black

Bright Red

Indian Yellow

Dark Sienna

Yellow Ochre

Prussian Blue

Sap Green

Phthalo Blue

Phthalo Green

ART DEFINITIONS

Alla Prima (**wet-on-wet**)—a painting technique where artists place oil paint on top of background layers without allowing the paint to dry first. In Italian, "alla prima" means "first attempt."

Canvas—a traditional painting canvas is usually a strong cloth that has been bleached, treated, and stretched over a wooden frame. A canvas is where an artist applies their paint.

Easel—a support used to hold a canvas upright at an angle. Easels help keep a canvas in place while an artist draws or paints.

Paintbrush—a brush used to apply paint. There are many different types of paint brushes. Bob Ross was known for using a large 2-inch brush to create his colorful backgrounds. He also used fan brushes, smaller brushes, and painting knives.

Painting knife—a tool used for mixing and applying paint. A painting knife can be plastic or metal and comes in different shapes—pointy and angular to blunt and round.

Palette—a board or object where an artist lays and mixes their paints. Traditional palettes are made of wood or plastic, are semi-circular, and can easily be held in one hand by an artist.

QUOTES CITED

In addition to the sources cited in the bibliography, quotes from this book were taken from the following episodes of *The Joy of Painting*:

The Joy of Painting, episode 201, "Meadow Lake," aired August 31, 1983, on WIPB in Muncie, Indiana.

The Joy of Painting, episode 202, "Winter Sun," aired September 7, 1983, on WIPB in Muncie, Indiana.

The Joy of Painting, episode 205, "Autumn Splendor," aired September 28, 1983 on WIPB in Muncie, Indiana.

The Joy of Painting, episode 207, "Brown Mountain," aired October 12, 1983, on WIPB in Muncie, Indiana.

The Joy of Painting, episode 212, "Mountain Waterfall," aired November 16, 1983, on WIPB in Muncie, Indiana.

The Joy of Painting, episode 305, "Distant Hills," aired February 1, 1984, on WIPB in Muncie, Indiana.

The Joy of Painting, episode 1113, "Happy Accident," aired March 25, 1987, on WIPB in Muncie, Indiana.

The Joy of Painting, episode 2306, "River's Peace," aired October 8, 1991, on WIPB in Muncie, Indiana.

The Joy of Painting, episode 3002, "Woodgrain View," aired November 30, 1993, on WIPB in Muncie, Indiana.

The Joy of Painting, episode 3103, "Winding Stream," aired March 8, 1994, on WIPB in Muncie, Indiana.

SELECT BIBLIOGRAPHY

Archer, S. "In Search of Sleep, With Bob Ross." The New Yorker, June 21, 2018. https://www.newyorker.com/culture/culture-desk/in-search-of-sleep-with-bob-ross

Bob Ross, Inc. (n.d.). Retrieved from Bob Ross: https://www.bobross.com/

Hajek, D. "The Real Bob Ross: Meet the Meticulous Artist Behind Those Happy Trees." NPR, August 19, 2016. https://www.npr.org/2016/08/29/490923502/the-real-bob-ross-meet-the-meticulous-artist-behind-those-happy-trees

Shrieves, L. "Bob Ross Uses His Brush To Spread Paint and Joy." The Orlando Sentinel, July 7, 1990. https://www.orlandosentinel.com/news/os-xpm-1990-07-07-9007060122-story.html

Spradlin, S., dir. Bob Ross: The Happy Painter 2011; Roanoke, VA: Blue Ridge PBS, 2011.

Stanley, A. "Bob Ross, the Frugal Gourmet of Painting." The New York Times, December 22, 1991. https://www.nytimes.com/1991/12/22/arts/television-bob-ross-the-frugal-gourmet-of-painting.html

Wilson, S. "'I think Florida was always his love': Happy little memories of Bob Ross' Central Florida roots." WFTV9, ABC, August 2, 2019. https://www.wftv.com/news/local/i-think-florida-was-always-his-love-happy-little-memories-of-bob-ross-central-florida-roots/950013890/